LIVE AND LOVE

OUT LOUD

**7 tips to transform your life
from busy and overwhelmed**

By: Tamara Robinson

Just to say **THANK YOU**

for purchasing this book,

here's my **FREE gift** to you

to help you on your journey

from busy and overwhelmed to a

focused and productive life.

www.FocusOnYouFreeGift.com

TABLE OF CONTENTS

INTRODUCTION

You picked up this book today, and like many other books that you've determined you're going to read before you ever opened the front page, you were already living as I had lived my life – overwhelmed. You're not sure if you're ever going to have time to deal with another thing or another task. Burning inside of you, you know there's more to do. You want so badly to live your life, to love out loud, but how do you do this? You're busy and overwhelmed. You're a mom, and you have a child that needs your time and attention. I know what it's like because I've been there. I want to share with you the incredible, miraculous breakthrough that God has brought into my life so that you can authentically be the best you can be in this world and love living your life out loud.

THE LIFE I DIDN'T CHOOSE

I remember 7 years ago when my divorce was finalizing, and I was coming out of a situation where I'd been both emotionally and verbally abused and overwhelmed. I was a single mom with a 5-year-old to raise, all alone without enough money to make ends meet. My lowest point was when I went to check my bank account and realized that I only had a total of $20 to cover me and my daughter's needs until my next pay day, which was two weeks away. I remember going to the dollar store to buy some groceries. I was trying to figure out what 10 items I could buy to cook something that will last for the next 2 weeks. I reserved the other $10 for gas for my car. That was not the way I wanted to live my life. I had to fight and change the situations where I'm in without losing me. I needed to learn that all of my focus couldn't be on just raising my daughter. I had to live my life too. I had to learn how to come from the lowest of situations to a place where I could live and love out loud on purpose.

There must be something more. You know how it is. Your child is so special and important to you, and you live in that constant place of guilt. I was not supposed to focus on me, so I kept neglecting myself. We keep on pushing ourselves to another day and in truth. We're really doing a disservice not only to ourselves but also to our children. Until we learn how to take care of ourselves first, we won't ever really be able to give all that we can give to our children. We won't be able to fulfill the call that is a part of living our life. It's important for each of us to know that we need to operate in our lane. We have to be the person that we were created to be because each of us was put on this earth with a specific space to fill and a role that only we can do.

SECOND CHANCE AT LIFE

You have a perfect example of that in your life. If you put down this book right now and look at one of your children, I guarantee you that the first thought that will come through your head is all of the things that you can see that they have potential in. The same is true for you. You're here for a specific reason. When you're not walking in your purpose, you're not complete, and you're not fulfilled. There are many things that we say to ourselves that we feel are important, but those are not necessarily what God put us here to do. We have to learn to be comfortable in our own skin. As one of my mentors, Nicole Roberts Jones always reminds me, "There's a gift in you!" I know there's a gift to you as well and the world is waiting for you to share it.

I remember when I was in college I got into a car accident. I got hit by a semi-truck, and I lived through it. I kept asking God Why He saved me. At the time, I didn't feel like I was worth it. That was because I didn't know my purpose. But what I learned is that I'm here because I was meant to do something. That's why I wrote this book. I want you to learn the things that you can do to live and love out loud.

You will find that there are six specific actions that you can take that will radically and dramatically change the course and the opportunity of your life, so that you can ultimately answer the call of who you were meant to be.

SEVEN ACTIONS TO TAKE TO CHANGE THE COURSE OF YOUR LIFE

FIRST: Meditation and Prayer

Prayer is you talking to God. Meditation is you listening and being open to what God is saying. I consider prayer and meditation together to truly be a full conversation with God because if I just talk, then I don't hear. There needs to be a time when I'm quiet and let God talk to me. I have learned that what I need to do first thing in the morning before I get out of bed is set the alarm. I spend the first 15 to 20 minutes in my bed just meditating and being open and quiet before God and allowing him to speak to me. This helps me find clarity and leaves me grounded and focused for the day. Praying and meditating gives me strength, through my connection to God, to do the things that

I need to do to excel. Rather than rushing into my day, I can start it off slowly with intention and purpose.

Prayer, on the other hand, is something that I do every day. Yes, there are times when I sneak away and pray about certain things in depth. But mostly, it's just a matter of communicating with God throughout the course of my day just like what you normally do with everybody else. I love to end my days praying as I go to sleep. Without prayer, I don't really know what I would have in this life. I encourage you to take up prayer and meditation as the first step to start your day to live a better life.

SECOND: Record your Thoughts (Journaling/Blogging)

What are the things that we receive in our meditation? How can I express the inner me? I found that exercises like writing, journaling, and blogging are so impactful and so important because it allows me to let everything that's going on inside of my head out. I like to write poetry. I found it to be very therapeutic throughout the difficult times in my life. I learned that poetry could help me put my emotions down on paper, and then as I read it back, I realize the things that I've been hiding from. Often the emotions inside of us are like a wall blocking us, keeping us from taking the next step. As we write these things out, it's like tearing down that wall brick by brick and being able to see the possibilities of living life on the other side of that wall. For me, after journaling for a while, I started blogging. I thought blogging would be my way to share these things with others, but it's really just like journaling, recording my thoughts, and expressing myself just on a different platform. It allows you to be able to identify the things that are keeping you from moving forward, so you can then deal with them and move forward in living your life.

THIRD: Self-care

This one was very difficult for me. I remember when my daughter was just a baby. A good friend of mine told me that when a baby takes a nap, you need to nap also. That seemed crazy to me. I shouldn't be taking a nap. What I should be doing are my chores. I need to wash the dishes, clean my baby's milk bottles, and all the other things that I am not able to do when the baby is awake. I didn't really see the point of taking a nap. I couldn't understand how I can take the time to nap while the baby's napping. However, I learned that if I take care of myself and choose to nap while my baby's asleep, then I'll have enough rest to take care of her when she wakes up. Resting, relaxing, taking me time and having downtime are the things that we can do to value ourselves. I can teach my daughter more on how to take care of herself by taking care of myself.

My flow is enhanced when I take care of myself. It doesn't just involve naps but many other things. I consider movement as one of my self-care techniques. With all of the years I've spent learning and practicing how to dance, I fell in love with it. I would turn on some music and dance around the house with my daughter. Even though we're doing it together, it's a wonderful form of letting go of the stress in your life. It's a great way to have fun as an adult. Sometimes I think that when we get to a certain age, we forget that we're allowed to have fun too.

And then there's food. Recently I completed a 21-day vegan reset. I'm not a vegan, but I lived a vegan lifestyle for 21 days for this particular exercise. I learned so much about myself during that time. I had a different approach to everything I ate, and that helped me focus on other things that I wasn't normally seeing. As I reset myself internally, I found that I wanted to reset my environment externally as well by cleaning things and clearing out things in my surroundings that I couldn't seem to deal with until I took this time to focus. It's important for us to eat right and take good care of ourselves.

The hardest one in self-care is learning how to give ourselves permission to enjoy the things that we love. It's so easy to put the things that we want to do on the back burner, especially for our children's sake. There are always so many things that they've got going on and days, weeks or months can go by without us ever taking any time for ourselves. What we really need to include as a part of our lives is the permission and the action of enjoying our own lives too. As we do, just like what my daughter said to me, they can see the difference when you're also happy in your life.

I want to encourage you not to feel bad about self-care for it's not selfish. I know as a people pleaser that I often find myself being so concerned about taking care of everybody else, that it was hard for me to learn to give myself permission to put myself first. Every time I'm on a plane I think of this because they always remind you that in the case of emergencies you need to put on your mask first before helping others. That applies to our lives too. You won't be able to help other people unless you help yourself first. If you don't, you won't have anything to give to other people.

FOURTH: Negative Chatter Doesn't Matter

This can come from other people, but most often than not, the person who's the loudest and most negative about yourself is YOU. I have always been my biggest critic. I hear God's voice, but then I wondered if it was really Him who was speaking. I'm not trying to reverse a message from God, but I often get in the way of what He's telling me to do because I focus on my own negative thoughts rather than the words that He's saying to me. We have to learn how to ignore our words and the words of others because the most loving and most meaningful people in our lives often say some of the most hurtful things.

I remember one time at church I was sharing with a minister that I wanted to write a book. He said, "Who do you think you are? You are not a leader. You shouldn't be writing a book." This made me doubt myself. I put off writing this book and the people it could've helped because a minister told me it was something I didn't have the right to do. I believed him because after all he was a church leader. What he said made me run from the things that I was supposed to be doing for so long. Like I said before, the people who are closest to us are often the ones who hurt us the most because they do not know how to support us. Our dreams, our goals, and our passions are not theirs. Just because these people don't understand our dreams, doesn't mean that it's something that can't or shouldn't happen.

I've been told by people that I smile too much. They said that I was always happy and too positive about everything. I don't know how else to be. It's not my fault that I can always see the possibility in things. Whenever a friend asks me for advice, I would tell them just to look at the opportunity in a positive way. Sometimes this response annoys my friends because what they really wanted is to have someone who would get angry with them about their situation. I'm sorry, but I am happy to smile all the time and surround my life with positivity. If you're just like me, I want to let you know that this is alright. The negative chatters of other people don't matter. Also, I spent too many years of my life feeling sad, lonely and depressed. Now that I've reconnected to my Divine purpose, I love smiling because it is authentically coming from the inside out.

One of my mentors, TeeJ Mercer, said in a video seminar she was doing recently that sometimes you are trying to fly, flapping your wings and there are things keeping you on the ground. Sometimes you just have to kick off those things in order to fly. For you to soar, you should ignore and leave in the past the negative chatter of others. When we listen to what God tells us, and then we're headed in the right direction. That's what we need to do and focus on. In life, we need to keep on moving forward. Not everyone will support us, but that's okay. Quiet that voice inside your head that's trying to give you all the reasons why it can't happen. Ignore the outside voices of the people because negative chatter doesn't matter.

FIFTH: Goal Setting

We need to have goals. Goal setting is imperative because if you don't know what you're going after, then you don't know whether you've reached it or not. Goals are things that you don't always share. Sometimes goals are not totally clear, but you don't really need anybody else's opinion on what to do. Once I went through these four steps that I've talked to you about, I realized that there are things that I need to accomplish. As I let the negative chatter go away, I realized that I was here for a purpose. I needed to stop putting myself on the back burner, and I needed to focus on the best and most authentic version of myself because even if we do put things on the back burner, those things that we are created to be will never go away. In order to do this, we have to come out of our comfort zone. We have to write down the goals that we want to accomplish in life. We need to create a situation for ourselves where our comfort zone is no longer comfortable and where we say to ourselves, "I can't stay here and reach my goals."

For a goal to be effective, it needs to be something that isn't impossible but will stretch you. Living out loud means being the best version of YOU, and your comfort zone is what usually gets in the way. We create authentic goals of who we are and what we need to do and then begin to start the process of doing what we're created to be. However, having a goal does not mean that everything in your life is going to be happy, but we can learn from those moments and how to take the goals that we've set in our lives and use each circumstance to help us create the life that we're meant to live.

SIXTH: Connection with Others

You need to come out of hiding. I was living in the world, but I was afraid to be myself and show who I really am because of my limiting beliefs. I told myself who I was and I thought everyone, including God, saw me that way. Eventually, I had to say to myself that I need to get over that. I need to be that person that God wants me to be. To do this, we have to surround ourselves with people who are like-minded. It's very hard to live a different kind of life and hang out with the people who are okay with having less in life. Surrounding ourselves with people who can contribute to our betterment will help us grow alongside with them. We will have a safe circle of people who are headed on the same path as we are. So I encourage you to reach out. When you find groups that feel like home and that have a coach or a leader, grab that opportunity so someone can help you take each step as you grow. If you're looking for a group to support you, I invite you to join my Focus on You Movement Facebook group for busy moms (www.focusonyoumovement.com).

All of this can be very challenging and difficult. Each of these six things is something that is easy for us to make excuses about. For me, as a single mom, I always had this sexy excuse that my daughter needs to go to school, to her dance class, etc. I was busy making excuses for not being me. We often say that we can't do it because we don't have the ability to invest in something, but what we don't understand is that we can start with free content or free groups that will help us figure out a way to invest in our future so that we can do better and go deeper in the things that we are called to do.

Some of the things that I've outlined here are going to take work. They are going to create new habits and patterns in your life. I remember when I started meditating, getting up twenty minutes earlier than I normally do was so hard. It was hard because it was something that we don't really want to do, but we have to make it a habit. As we set that alarm and get up that fifteen or twenty minutes earlier, we will slowly move from a place of struggling every day to go back to sleep to a place where we start looking forward to our mornings listening to God. Things will start to get better as we listen more to His voice and not the negative chatter. I can promise you that after the first thirty days of meditating in the morning, it does get a lot easier. Now, I wake up early in the morning feeling alive.

Now, here's the last excuse that I've also used in the past so many times, "I'm a single parent/dad/mom." It's such an easy label to use as a crutch. It's a great thing that we can throw in the way of the opportunities in our life to hold us back from being all that we can be. But whether married or single, whether we have someone in our lives to help us or not, we can't fall into the excuse of believing that just because we are single moms or dads we're not meant for anything else. Before that child was born, we were already created for a purpose.

SEVENTH: Answer the Call

I challenge you to answer the call. How? It's simple and hard at the same time – TAKE ACTION. Take the things that I've shared with you and do something with it. I can tell you from experience that once I started doing all of these things, there was something inside of me that was awakened. As I began to pay attention and focus on being who I really am, I felt so alive. My eyes were opened to the reality that there was more to me. It started to become clear on why I was in this world in the first place. We should not conform to what others are telling us to do. Just like what Lisa Nichols said, "Maybe I'm a unicorn. Maybe I wasn't meant to fit in." Fitting in in life won't give you a sense of fulfillment.

As we surround ourselves more and more with people that are wanting to grow, we will find that we can do more. As for me, I've realized that I am here to help other single moms to find and live their inner dreams. I want to help them fulfill those desires and pursue the best version of themselves without guilt. I encourage you not to buy into that story that we are supposed to grow up, go to college, and be this or that person. Just be the person you are created to be.

Creating this book and sharing with you all of these things is me answering my call in life, and that's what I want you to do as well – answer your call in life. Live and love out loud.

ANSWER THE CALL

By Tamara Robinson

Answer the call towards the vision &
mission God has placed on your life
When you hear God's voice calling you
to action, this is definitely not the time
to run away or hide

When God says move you can trust &
believe it means to move and not just
sit around and talk

And when the time comes to make
some changes, God will let you know
exactly when & where to walk

God will prepare the way for you &
order your steps as you obey & follow
His lead

As the soil is watered, God will provide
the increase, but first, you must plant
the seed

God gives us commands toward our
destiny that are plain, basic, & simple

God wants to be certain that before we're blessed with much, we can be trusted with little

So don't fear the call that's placed on your life, just accept it & walk towards it in faith

And listen for God to provide answers to your questions that may come up along the way

In order to know you are correctly hearing the voice of the Almighty, you must read & study God's Word

Or you'll end up confused like Samuel & not know the originating voice of the command you just heard

The first three times he heard his name, Samuel thought it was Eli, but then we read in 1 Samuel 3:10

Where he properly answered the call by finally saying, "Speak Lord for your servant is listening."

We can also read in God's Word where it says that faith without works is dead

So it's time to take action & step out on faith and accomplish the tasks that God has placed in your head

And don't look around at what's going on in your life or try to force this task into your current situation

Because the excuse or situation you're putting so much focus on is actually a training ground for your next destination

You've been thinking & talking a lot lately about what you're going to do

But now is the time to just do it, get the job done, & stop waiting around for another clue

So don't waste any more time worrying about the future or about what will come up next

Once you answer the call & take that first step, God will be right there to guide you through the rest.

LET'S CONNECT

Email: info@tamararobinson.net

Facebook group for busy and overwhelmed moms: www.FocusOnYouMovement.com

Twitter: @TamaraLatrese

(If you've read this book, I want you to write, "@TamaraLatrese I'm ready to Live and Love Out Loud")

(use hashtags #LiveandLovebook, #FocusOnYouMovement)